LIGHTNING
BOLT
BOOKS™

Let's Visit the Grassland

Jennifer Boothroyd

Lerner Publications • Minneapolis

For the
Palmisano family

Lerner Publications Company
A division of Lerner Publishing Group, Inc.
241 First Avenue North
Minneapolis, MN 55401 USA

For reading levels and more information, look up this title at www.lernerbooks.com.

Library of Congress Cataloging-in-Publication Data

Names: Boothroyd, Jennifer, 1972- author.
Title: Let's visit the grassland / Jennifer Boothroyd.
Other titles: Let us visit the grassland
Description: Minneapolis : Lerner Publications, [2017] | Series: Lightning bolt books. Biome explorers |
    Audience: Ages 5-8. | Audience: K to grade 3. | Includes bibliographical references and index.
Identifiers: LCCN 2015048775 (print) | LCCN 2016002248 (ebook) | ISBN 9781512411928 (lb : alk.
    paper) | ISBN 9781512412307 (pb : alk. paper) | ISBN 9781512412000 (eb pdf)
Subjects: LCSH: Grassland ecology—Juvenile literature. | Grassland animals—Juvenile literature.
Classification: LCC QH541.5.P7 B66 2017 (print) | LCC QH541.5.P7 (ebook) | DDC 577.4—dc23

LC record available at http://lccn.loc.gov/2015048775

Manufactured in the United States of America
1-39694-21305-3/22/2016

Table of Contents

A Journey to the Grassland

Tall plants sway as the wind blows gently. The mostly flat grassland stretches far into the distance.

This area is buzzing with activity. Insects, birds, and other animals can find food and shelter in the grassland.

Grassland biomes are found around the world. They can be tropical or temperate. Temperate grasslands in North America are known as the prairie.

This map shows temperate grasslands around the world.

NORTH AMERICA

EUROPE

ASIA

AFRICA

SOUTH AMERICA

AUSTRALIA

Grassland

ANTARCTICA

In winter, the prairie can be freezing cold and covered in snow.

Trees like this baobab
grow in tropical grasslands.

Tropical grasslands are very
different from the prairie.
They are warm year-round.
It rains a lot during the
rainy season. It is dry the
rest of the year.

Fire is important to all grasslands. Fire removes old plants, kills nonnative plants, and brings nutrients to the soil. The roots of native prairie plants can survive a fire.

Animals in the Grassland

American bison graze on prairie grass. They can grow more than 6 feet (1.8 meters) tall. That's taller than many people. Bison have thick hides that keep them warm in cold winters.

Pronghorns travel the prairie in herds. Both male and female pronghorns shed their horns each year. They use their hooves to get to grass beneath the snow.

Red-tailed hawks circle high over fields or perch on telephone poles to watch for prey.

Red-tailed hawks soar high above the prairie. They hunt animals such as mice, rabbits, and snakes.

A killdeer makes a nest on the prairie's ground. To protect its nest, it tricks predators by pretending to have a broken wing. The predator follows the bird away from its nest. The killdeer flies back once the predator has moved away.

Garter snakes slither through the prairie grass. They eat small animals such as mice and toads. They hibernate underground during cold winter weather.

A grasshopper's coloring helps it hide from predators.

A prairie's grasshoppers spring from plant to plant. These insects have long back legs and two pairs of wings. They jump or fly to get away from predators.

Grasshoppers also live in tropical grasslands. Tropical grasslands in Africa are home to elephants and zebras too!

Plants in the Grassland

The prairie is full of many kinds of plants. Some are tall, and some are short. Wildflowers bloom in spring, summer, and fall.

Dry weather means few trees grow in the prairie. Some trees grow along riverbanks.

Monarch butterflies in the prairie depend on milkweed. They lay their eggs on the plants. Caterpillars hatch from the eggs and eat the milkweed before becoming butterflies.

Big bluestem grass is one of the tallest prairie plants. Its roots grow deep into the ground. In spring, it has tiny yellow flowers. Many prairie animals eat big bluestem.

The wind is very important to bluejoint grass. The wind helps pollinate the plant. It also carries the plant's seeds around the prairie.

Grasses also grow in tropical grasslands. Tropical grasslands have some trees as well. The acacia and jackalberry are two common trees in tropical grasslands.

This acacia tree grows on a tropical grassland.

Important Connections

All life is connected on the prairie. Prairie dogs are one of the most important parts of prairie ecosystems!

Black-footed ferrets rely on prairie dogs for food. The ferrets are endangered. Without prairie dogs, the ferrets may die out.

Some people think prairie dogs are pests because they dig. But their digging can be helpful!

Prairie dogs dig burrows underground. Their digging mixes the soil and gives it air. This helps plants grow.

Some animals rely on prairie dog burrows for shelter. Snakes and burrowing owls live in old prairie dog burrows.

Prairie dogs are just one example of how prairie plants and animals are linked. Links like these help keep the prairie healthy and thriving.

People in the Prairie

People have lived in the prairie for thousands of years. American Indians followed the bison herds. They used prairie plants for food and medicine. Later, European pioneers turned much of the grassland into farmland. Recently, people have been working hard to return old farmland to prairie land. They plant native seeds and carefully burn areas to remove nonnative prairie plants. They limit hunting and trapping to protect the animals in the habitat.

Biome Extremes

- Largest unplowed prairie in the United States: Kansas Flint Hills, 11,400 square miles (29,525 square kilometers)

- Heaviest land animal native to North America: American bison, 930 to 2,200 pounds (422 to 998 kilograms)

- Fastest land animal native to North America: pronghorn, 53 miles (86 km) per hour

- Largest prairie dog town: discovered in Texas in 1901, 25,000 square miles (65,000 sq. km), with an estimated population of four hundred million prairie dogs

- Tallest prairie grass: a few prairie grasses can grow more than 10 feet (3 m) tall, including big bluestem grass and Indian grass

Glossary

biome: plants and animals in a large area, such as a desert or forest

ecosystem: an area of connected living and nonliving things

endangered: in danger of dying out completely

grassland: a large open area covered by grass and other plants but with few trees

herd: a group of hoofed animals that stay together

hibernate: to spend winter in a deep sleep

native: starting in a specific location

nutrient: something a plant or animal needs to grow and survive

pollinate: to move pollen from one plant to another

predator: an animal that hunts and eats other animals

Further Reading

Anderson, Sheila. *What Can Live in a Grassland?* Minneapolis: Lerner Publications, 2011.

Fleisher, Paul. *Grassland Food Webs in Action.* Minneapolis: Lerner Publications, 2014.

Johansson, Philip. *The Grasslands: Discover This Wide Open Biome.* Berkeley Heights, NJ: Enslow, 2015.

Kids Do Ecology: World Biomes
http://kids.nceas.ucsb.edu/biomes/grassland.html

Minnesota's Biomes
http://www.dnr.state.mn.us/biomes/prairie.html

National Geographic: Grasslands
http://environment.nationalgeographic.com/environment/habitats/grassland-profile

Index

Photo Acknowledgments

The images in this book are used with the permission of: © Ken Schulze/Shutterstock.com, p. 2; © Mark Baldwin/Shutterstock.com, p. 4; © Todd Klassy/Shutterstock.com, p. 5; © Laura Westlund/Independent Picture Service, p. 6; © SNEHIT/Shutterstock.com, p. 7; © Ann Cantelow/Shutterstock.com, p. 8; © Dennis van de Water/Shutterstock.com, p. 9; © Photoshot License Ltd/Alamy, p. 10; © IrinaK/Shutterstock.com, p. 11; © Jeffery B. Banks/Shutterstock.com, p. 12; © Phoo Chan/Shutterstock.com, p. 13; © Menno Schaefer/Shutterstock.com, p. 14; © Jason Patrick Ross/Shutterstock.com, p. 15; © Pairoj Sroyngem/Shutterstock.com, p. 16; © Andrezej Kubik/Shutterstock.com, p. 17; © Jason Patrick Ross/Shutterstock.com, p. 18; © iStockphoto.com/genesisgraphics, p. 19; © Clint Frarlinger/Alamy, p. 20; © age fotostock/Alamy, p. 21; © Maciej Czekajewski/Shutterstock.com, p. 22; © Henk Bentlage/Shutterstock.com, pp. 23, 31; © All Canada Photos/Alamy, p. 24; © ValEs1989/Shutterstock.com, p. 25; © David Nagy/Shutterstock.com, p. 26; © Dlogger/Shutterstock.com, p. 27.

Front cover: © Mark Baldwin/Shutterstock.com.

Main body text set in Johann Light 30/36.